Written by
Collene Dobelmann

Editors: Regina Hurh Kim/Janet Sweet
Cover Illustrator: Rick Grayson
Cover Designer: Rebekah O. Lewis
Art Director: Moonhee Pak
Project Director: Stacey Faulkner

Table of Contents

Introduction **3**

How to Use This Book **4**

Minute Journal **6**

Scope and Sequence **7**

Grammar Minutes **8**

Answer Key **108**

Introduction

The main objective of *Grammar Minutes Grade 6* is grammar proficiency, attained by teaching students to apply grammar skills to answer questions effortlessly and rapidly. The questions in this book provide students with practice in the following key areas of sixth-grade grammar instruction:

- nouns and pronouns
- verb forms and verb tenses
- adjectives and adverbs
- prepositional phrases
- contractions
- compound and complex sentences
- appositives and clauses

- word usage
- synonyms, antonyms, and homophones
- noun and pronoun agreement
- subject and verb agreement
- prefixes and suffixes
- Greek and Latin roots

Use this comprehensive resource to improve your students' overall grammar proficiency, which will promote greater self-confidence in their grammar skills as well as provide the everyday practice necessary to succeed in testing situations.

Grammar Minutes Grade 6 features 100 "Minutes." Each Minute consists of 10 questions for students to complete within a short time period. As students are becoming familiar with the format of the Minutes, they may need more time to complete each one. Once they are comfortable and familiar with the format, give students a one- to two-minute period to complete each Minute. The quick, timed format, combined with instant feedback, makes this a challenging and motivational assignment that offers students an ongoing opportunity to improve their own proficiency in a manageable, nonthreatening way.

How to Use This Book

Grammar Minutes Grade 6 is designed to generally progress through the skills as they are introduced in the classroom in sixth grade. The Minutes can be implemented in either numerical order, starting with Minute 1, or in any order based on your students' specific needs during the school year. The complexity of the sentences and the tasks within each skill being covered gradually increase so that the first Minute of a skill is generally easier than the second Minute on the same skill. Review lessons are included throughout the book, as well as in an application section at the end of the book.

Grammar Minutes Grade 6 can be used in a variety of ways. Use one Minute a day as a warm-up activity, skill review, assessment, test prep, extra credit assignment, or homework assignment. Keep in mind that students will get the most benefit from each Minute if they receive immediate feedback.

If you use the Minute as a timed activity, begin by placing the paper facedown on the students' desks or displaying it as a transparency. Use a clock or kitchen timer to measure one minute—or more if needed. As the Minutes become more advanced, use your discretion on extending the time frame to several minutes if needed. Encourage students to concentrate on completing each question successfully and not to dwell on questions they cannot complete. At the end of the allotted time, have the students stop working. Read the answers from the answer key (pages 108–112) or display them on a transparency. Have students correct their own work and record their scores on the Minute Journal reproducible (page 6). Then have the class go over each question together to discuss the answers. Spend more time on questions that were clearly challenging for most of the class. Tell students that some skills that seemed difficult for them will appear again on future Minutes and that they will have another opportunity for success.

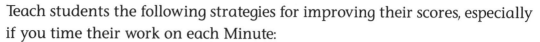

Teach students the following strategies for improving their scores, especially if you time their work on each Minute:

- leave more challenging items for last
- come back to items they are unsure of after they have completed all other items
- make educated guesses when they encounter items with which they are unfamiliar
- ask questions if they are still unsure about anything

Students will ultimately learn to apply these strategies to other assignments and testing situations.

The Minutes are designed to assess and improve grammar proficiency and should not be included as part of a student's overall language arts grade. However, the Minutes provide an excellent opportunity to identify which skills the class as a whole needs to practice or review. Use this information to plan the content of future grammar lessons. For example, if many students in the class have difficulty with a Minute on commas, additional lessons in that area will be useful and valuable for the students' future success.

While Minute scores will not be included in students' formal grades, it is important to recognize student improvements by offering individual or class rewards and incentives for scores above a certain level on a daily and/or weekly basis. Showing students recognition for their efforts provides additional motivation to succeed.

Minute Journal

Name _____

Minute	Date	Score	Minute	Date	Score	Minute	Date	Score	Minute	Date	Score
1			26			51			76		
2			27			52			77		
3			28			53			78		
4			29			54			79		
5			30			55			80		
6			31			56			81		
7			32			57			82		
8			33			58			83		
9			34			59			84		
10			35			60			85		
11			36			61			86		
12			37			62			87		
13			38			63			88		
14			39			64			89		
15			40			65			90		
16			41			66			91		
17			42			67			92		
18			43			68			93		
19			44			69			94		
20			45			70			95		
21			46			71			96		
22			47			72			97		
23			48			73			98		
24			49			74			99		
25			50			75			100		

Grammar Minutes · Grade 6 © 2009 Creative Teaching Press

Scope and Sequence

MINUTE	SKILL	MINUTE	SKILL
1	Complete and Incomplete Sentences	49	Dependent Clauses
2	Types of Sentences	50	Independent Clauses
3	Simple and Complete Subjects and Predicates	51	Commas
4	Common Nouns	52	Compound Sentences
5	Common and Proper Nouns	53	Complex Sentences
6	Plural Nouns	54	Compound-Complex Sentences
7	More Plural Nouns	55	Conjunctions Review
8	Singular Possessive Nouns	56	Compound Subjects and Compound Predicates Review
9	Plural Possessive Nouns	57	Prepositions and Prepositional Phrases Review
10	Subject and Object Pronouns	58	Dependent and Independent Clauses Review
11	Complete Sentences and End Punctuation Review	59	Compound, Complex, and Compound-Complex Sentences Review
12	Common and Proper Nouns Review	60	Appositives
13	Singular and Plural Nouns Review	61	More Uses for Commas
14	Possessive Nouns Review	62	Quotation Marks
15	Subject and Object Pronouns Review	63	Contractions
16	Action Verbs	64	Abbreviations
17	Linking Verbs	65	Semicolons
18	Helping Verbs	66	Colons
19	Past, Present, and Future Tense Verbs	67	Word Usage: Sit or Set
20	Perfect Tense Verbs	68	Word Usage: Lie or Lay
21	Irregular Verbs	69	Word Usage: Your or You're
22	Progressive Verbs	70	Appositives Review
23	Transitive Verbs	71	Commas and Quotations Review
24	Intransitive Verbs	72	Contractions and Abbreviations Review
25	Subject and Verb Agreement	73	Colons and Semicolons Review
26	Action Verbs Review	74	Word Usage Review
27	Linking and Helping Verbs Review	75	Interjections
28	Verb Tenses Review	76	Articles
29	Verb Forms Review	77	Prefixes
30	Subject and Verb Agreement Review	78	Suffixes
31	Adjectives	79	More Prefixes
32	Comparative and Superlative Adjectives	80	More Suffixes
33	Irregular Comparative and Superlative Adjectives	81	Greek Root Words
34	Adverbs	82	Latin Root Words
35	More Adverbs	83	Spelling Patterns and Exceptions
36	Adverbs without -ly	84	More Spelling Patterns and Exceptions
37	Synonyms	85	Negatives
38	Antonyms	86	Interjections and Articles Review
39	Homophones	87	Prefixes Review
40	Adjectives Review	88	Suffixes Review
41	Comparative and Superlative Adjectives Review	89	Greek and Latin Root Words Review
42	Adverbs Review	90	Spelling Patterns and Exceptions Review
43	Synonyms and Antonyms Review	91	Negatives Review
44	Homophones Review	92–100	Apply Your Grammar Knowledge
45	Conjunctions		
46	Compound Subjects		
47	Compound Predicates		
48	Prepositions and Prepositional Phrases		

Scope and Sequence

Minute 1

Name _____

Write *C* if the sentence is complete or *I* if it is incomplete.

1. Michelle starts sixth grade at a new school on Friday. _____

2. Got to get school supplies. _____

3. Very nervous about the first day. _____

4. She hopes that she will make friends quickly. _____

5. Michelle's cousin attends the same school, but they won't have any classes together. _____

6. Heard that the history and science classes are hard. _____

7. Michelle will join the choir as soon as she can. _____

8. She enjoys singing. _____

9. Only three more days of summer vacation! _____

10. Michelle's cousin will show her around the school before the first day. _____

Grammar Minutes · Grade 6 © 2009 Creative Teaching Press

Minute 2

Name _____

Write the correct end punctuation (period, question mark, or exclamation point) for each sentence. Then write the type of sentence it is on the line: *declarative, interrogative, imperative, or exclamatory.*
(**Hint:** A *declarative* sentence is a statement. An *interrogative* sentence asks a question. An *imperative* sentence makes a request or a command. The "you" does not appear in the sentence but it is understood. An *exclamatory* sentence shows strong feeling.)

1. Timothy's first day of school was not bad___ _____

2. Have you ever been the new kid at school___ _____

3. I dropped my lunch tray. What an
   embarrassing moment___ _____

4. I slipped and fell, and my tray made
   a loud clatter___ _____

5. Did you hurt yourself___ _____

6. That is how I met my best friend___ _____

7. She said everyone has moments they would
   rather forget___ _____

8. Sit next to me___ _____

9. I am so ecstatic to finally have a friend___ _____

10. Tell me your most embarrassing moment___ _____

Types of Sentences

Minute 3

Name _____

For Numbers 1–5, circle the simple subject of each sentence. Underline the complete subject.
(**Hint:** The *simple subject* is the someone or something the sentence is about. The *complete subject* includes all words related to whom or what the sentence is about.)

1. Our eager classroom teacher began the lesson.

2. The yellow marker did not show up on the overhead projector.

3. The algebra problem was really difficult to solve.

4. The students, including my best friend, have English class after Algebra.

5. Do you have gym today?

For Numbers 6–10, circle the simple predicate for each sentence. Underline the complete predicate.
(**Hint:** The *simple predicate* is the action or linking verb without any other words that modify it or describe the subject. The *complete predicate* includes all words that show what the complete subject is or does.)

6. Ms. Linette asked Tyson to demonstrate how to solve the problem.

7. I solved the problem by working backwards.

8. My two classmates were the only ones to correctly answer the problem.

9. Several members of the class tried to work through the problem again.

10. Did anyone use a different method?

Grammar Minutes · Grade 6 © 2009 Creative Teaching Press

Minute 4

Name _____

Circle the two common nouns in each sentence.

1. Dylan and Shelby bought a puppy yesterday from the pound.

2. They can't think of a good name for their pet.

3. Shelby wanted to name the dog "Bubbles" and get its collar inscribed.

4. Dylan and Shelby got into an argument over their choices.

5. He thought of naming the puppy "Bear" because it looks like a bear.

6. Shelby did not want to get into a fight, but she disliked his suggestion.

7. Finally, their mother offered an alternative.

8. How about solving the problem by calling the hyper creature "Dash"?

9. "He does love to play chase," the kids noted.

10. Dylan and Shelby called to their new friend, who came running with his tail wagging.

Grammar Minutes · Grade 6 © 2009 Creative Teaching Press

Minute 5

Name _____

Circle the common noun(s) in each sentence. Underline any proper nouns that are missing capitalization, and rewrite them correctly on the lines. The number in parentheses tells how many total nouns you should circle or rewrite in each sentence.

1. My dog remy has a shaggy coat. (3) _____

2. I had to take Remy to see his groomer at furry friends grooming shop. (5) _____

3. He bathes Remy and brushes his fur. (1) _____

4. Another worker, henry, clips Remy's claws and cleans his ears. (4) _____

5. Remy likes to play with his friend trixie. (2) _____

6. She wears a pink collar around her neck. (2) _____

7. Henry rewards the dogs with treats for good behavior. (3) _____

8. The dogs lick Henry's hands and face enthusiastically. (3) _____

9. Then the canines are ready to go home. (2) _____

10. If you have a pet, take it to the shop on highland boulevard. (4) _____

Grammar Minutes · Grade 6 © 2009 Creative Teaching Press

Minute 6

Name _____

Circle the two plural nouns in each sentence.

1. Our cat had its babies on a bed of blankets yesterday.

2. Mom says our house has more pets than people.

3. She asked her coworkers and friends if any of them wanted a kitten.

4. Sandra said her twins have always wanted cats.

5. I found families for three more of the felines.

6. The kitten with orange and white patches, the gray kitten, and the white kitten still need homes.

7. She likes to settle on her haunches and then pounce at your toes when you least expect it!

8. Her favorite games are chasing my neighbor's puppy and playing with the leaves in the yard.

9. Luckily, my neighbors kept the orange and white kitten, and two women took the last two.

10. If I had two wishes, I would get to keep a kitten, and mom would get us dogs!

Plural Nouns

Minute 7

Name _____

Write the plural form for each noun.

1. church _____

2. tree _____

3. country _____

4. bus _____

5. baby _____

6. deer _____

7. shelf _____

8. goose _____

9. belief _____

10. child _____

Grammar Minutes · Grade 6 © 2009 Creative Teaching Press

Minute 8

Name _____

Write the singular possessive form to replace the underlined phrase in each sentence.

(**Hint:** A *singular possessive noun* shows ownership by one person or thing. Adding *'s* to a noun makes it possessive.)

1. The <u>toy that belongs to the dog</u> is under the couch. _____

2. Please give me the <u>bottle that belongs to the baby</u>. _____

3. Do you have <u>the baseball that belongs to Trevor</u>? _____

4. The <u>stinger of the bee</u> is sharp! _____

5. The <u>tail of the puppy</u> wagged and wagged. _____

6. The <u>wing of the bird</u> is not broken. _____

7. I like <u>the car that belongs to your mother</u>. _____

8. The <u>back tire of the bus</u> was flat. _____

9. The <u>tracks of that deer</u> led to the garden. _____

10. Have you seen <u>the new haircut of Mom</u>? _____

Grammar Minutes · Grade 6 © 2009 Creative Teaching Press

Singular Possessive Nouns

Minute 9

Name _____

Write the plural possessive form to replace the underlined phrase in each sentence.

(**Hint:** A *plural possessive noun* shows ownership by more than one person or thing. When a plural noun ends in *-s*, adding an apostrophe ['] to the end makes it possessive. Example: The room belonging to the sisters = sisters' room.)

1. The <u>uniforms that belong to the cheerleaders</u> are red and white. _____

2. The <u>helmets that belong to the football players</u> keep them safe. _____

3. The <u>horns that belong to the trumpeters</u> sound great. _____

4. Do you like the <u>performances of the marching bands?</u> _____

5. I can hear the <u>cheers of the people</u>. _____

6. The <u>coaches of the teams</u> are fired up about the game. _____

7. The <u>uniforms of the mascots</u> are hot and itchy. _____

8. The concession stand sells <u>cakes and pies made by the football parents</u>. _____

9. When it rains, it's hard to see over the <u>umbrellas belonging to the fans</u>. _____

10. The <u>taunts of the rivals</u> are all in good fun. _____

Grammar Minutes · Grade 6 © 2009 Creative Teaching Press

Minute 10

Name _____

For Numbers 1–5, write the correct subject pronoun from the box to complete each sentence. Not all pronouns will be used.

You	He	She	It	We	They

1. _____ won't ever forget your homework if you put it in your backpack right after finishing it.

2. Devin and Kendra are helpful tutors. _____ will always help their students with their homework.

3. _____ is often late to turn in his homework.

4. _____ never waits to do her homework until the last minute.

5. _____ do our homework together after school.

For Numbers 6–10, write the correct object pronoun from the box to replace the underlined word(s) in each sentence.

you	him	her	it	me	us	them

6. I bought new games, so I have to learn how to play <u>the games</u>. _____

7. We asked Mr. Mendoza to play a game with <u>Elizabeth, Brian, and me</u>. _____

8. Mr. Mendoza turned to Megan and asked <u>Megan</u> to play, too. _____

9. Brian said, "I don't know how to play. Will you teach <u>Brian</u>?" _____

10. Mr. Mendoza replied to Brian that he would be happy to teach <u>Brian</u>. _____

*Grammar Minutes · Grade 6* © 2009 Creative Teaching Press

Minute 11

Name _____

Read each sentence. If the sentence is incomplete, write *I*. If the sentence is complete, add the correct end punctuation mark.

1. Where would you like to spend your vacation___

2. Love going to Santa Barbara, California___

3. I have heard that the beaches are beautiful___

4. I can't wait to learn to surf___

5. My brothers and I have before___

6. I bought goggles and snorkels___

7. Are you comfortable in the water___

8. Yes, I like to swim___

9. When do you want to___

10. Is it time to pack yet___

Minute 12

Name _____

Underline the common noun(s) and circle any proper noun(s) in each sentence. The number in parentheses tells how many total nouns you should underline or circle.

1. Stephen visited Washington, D.C., last winter. (3)

2. He went with his grandfather and his cousin, Joseph. (3)

3. They visited the Washington Monument and the Lincoln Memorial. (2)

4. Papa Joe wanted to visit the Vietnam Veterans Memorial. (2)

5. They could see the dome of the United States Capitol from the National Mall. (3)

6. Stephen attends Gallaudet University in the city. (3)

7. Stephen and Joseph chatted excitedly as they walked along Pennsylvania Avenue. (3)

8. They took photos of the White House but did not see the president. (3)

9. Stephen had bought a small souvenir flag of the United States. (3)

10. Joseph bought postcards of the Oval Office and the *USS Philadelphia*. (4)

Grammar Minutes • Grade 6 © 2009 Creative Teaching Press

Common and Proper Nouns Review

Minute 13

Name _____

Write the singular or plural form for each noun.

Singular	Plural
1. person	_____
2. cherry	_____
3. _____	cacti
4. industry	_____
5. _____	sheep
6. _____	scarves
7. woman	_____
8. vertebra	_____
9. _____	parentheses
10. calf	_____

Grammar Minutes · Grade 6 © 2009 Creative Teaching Press

Minute 14

Name _____

For Numbers 1–5, circle *singular possessive* or *plural possessive* to describe the underlined words in each sentence.

1. The <u>islanders' boats</u> were long, slender rowboats.

   singular possessive   plural possessive

2. That <u>boat's markings</u> are different from the others.

   singular possessive   plural possessive

3. All the other <u>boats' paintings</u> are similar.

   singular possessive   plural possessive

4. A <u>man's voice</u> calls to the oarsmen.

   singular possessive   plural possessive

5. The <u>oarsmen's response</u> comes back loud and strong.

   singular possessive   plural possessive

For Numbers 6–10, write the plural possessive form for each phrase.

Singular Possessive	Plural Possessive
6. man's oars	_____
7. island's shore	_____
8. person's net	_____
9. tribe's custom	_____
10. wave's crest	_____

Grammar Minutes · Grade 6 © 2009 Creative Teaching Press

Possessive Nouns Review

Minute 15

Name _____

Write the correct pronoun from the box to replace the underlined noun in each sentence.

she	we	they	him	us

1. It's Dad's birthday. Mom bought <u>Dad</u> a new watch. _____

2. Our car broke down. Will you take <u>Keith and me</u> to school? _____

3. <u>Hannah</u> makes her own jewelry. _____

4. Our neighbors left, but <u>the neighbors</u> are coming back soon. _____

5. <u>My brothers and I</u> are throwing a party for my mother. _____

Write the correct pronoun from the box to complete each sentence. Use each pronoun only once.

you	I	it	he	them

6. Trey and Toni like sweets, so we brought _____ some cookies.

7. _____ look like you have seen a ghost!

8. The gardeners who were searching for the rabbit finally noticed _____ near the tree.

9. _____ brought him some of my homemade chicken soup.

10. _____ got in trouble for hitting his sister.

Grammar Minutes · Grade 6 © 2009 Creative Teaching Press

Minute 16

Name _____

Write your own action verbs to complete the paragraph. Use each verb only once.

Victoria wants to _____ a pie for dessert. Victoria _____ a list of groceries
                1.   2.
to buy. She throws the list in her purse and _____ to the store. She _____
                                     3.   4.
tart apples and _____ the flour, cinnamon, and sugar. Victoria _____ her
                5.   6.
items to the checkout stand. She _____ home immediately and _____ her
                                  7.   8.
work space. She carefully measures the ingredients. She _____ the recipe closely.
                                                              9.
Victoria's family _____ the pie with ice cream and savors every bite!
                      10.

1. _____   6. _____

2. _____   7. _____

3. _____   8. _____

4. _____   9. _____

5. _____   10. _____

Grammar Minutes · Grade 6 © 2009 Creative Teaching Press

Action Verbs

Minute 17

Name _____

Circle the linking verb in each sentence.
(**Hint**: A *linking verb* does not express action. It connects the subject to the rest of the information about the subject.)

1. Abel was sick on Friday.

2. He became queasy after lunch.

3. Ms. Grey said, "Abel, you seem feverish."

4. "I feel awful," he whispered.

5. "I am sorry!" responded Ms. Grey.

6. She added, "You'll be more comfortable in the nurse's office."

7. She and Abel's classmates were helpful.

8. The nurse told Abel, "Your mother is concerned. She'll pick you up soon."

9. "You are kind," said Abel.

10. "You'll feel well by Monday," said the nurse.

Grammar Minutes • Grade 6 © 2009 Creative Teaching Press

Minute 18

Name _____

Circle the helping verb in each sentence.
(**Hint:** A *helping verb* is used with another verb and expresses such things as person, number, mood, or tense.)

1. I am reading *Tuck Everlasting* by Natalie Babbitt.

2. My friends are reading it with me.

3. We have enjoyed it so far.

4. The main character, Winnie, is trying to decide if she wants to live forever.

5. My friends wondered what they might do in her situation.

6. I was thinking about the same thing.

7. I will ask my teacher if she thinks it is a good idea.

8. I think I would choose to live forever.

9. My teacher does agree with me.

10. She has pondered the question, too.

Grammar Minutes · Grade 6 © 2009 Creative Teaching Press

Helping Verbs

Minute 19

Name _____

Read each sentence and underline the verb or verb phrase. Then circle the verb tense: *past tense, present tense,* or *future tense.*

1. I do different chores every day after school.

    past tense   present tense   future tense

2. Yesterday I cleaned the rabbit's cage.

    past tense   present tense   future tense

3. I also helped Mom with dinner.

    past tense   present tense   future tense

4. Rene will help with the cooking tonight.

    past tense   present tense   future tense

5. She and Mom plan to make spaghetti and meatballs.

    past tense   present tense   future tense

6. I will water the grass and potted plants.

    past tense   present tense   future tense

7. I forgot to sweep the porch.

    past tense   present tense   future tense

8. I try to remember to take out the trash.

    past tense   present tense   future tense

9. I will get my allowance on Friday if all my chores are done.

    past tense   present tense   future tense

10. I save half of my allowance money for college.

    past tense   present tense   future tense

Grammar Minutes · Grade 6 © 2009 Creative Teaching Press

Minute 20

Name _____

Read each sentence and underline the perfect-tense verb phrase. Then circle the verb tense: *past perfect, present perfect,* or *future perfect.*
(**Hint:** Use the helping verb in each sentence to help you decide the tense.)

1. Mel had packed her suitcase.

       past perfect   present perfect   future perfect

2. She had planned an exciting summer vacation.

       past perfect   present perfect   future perfect

3. Mel will have canceled those plans by now.

       past perfect   present perfect   future perfect

4. Mel's friend has called to say he needs her help.

       past perfect   present perfect   future perfect

5. Dan has broken his leg.

       past perfect   present perfect   future perfect

For Numbers 6–10, complete the table with the correct form for each verb.

Past Perfect	Present Perfect	Future Perfect
6. had said	_____	_____
7. _____	_____	will have regretted
8. _____	has lounged	_____
9. _____	has assured	_____
10. had expressed	_____	_____

Perfect Tense Verbs

Minute 21

Name _____

Write the correct form for each verb to complete the table.
(Hint: *Irregular verbs* do not end in *–ed* in the past or past participle tenses.)

Present Tense	Past Tense	Past Participle
1. eat	_____	eaten
2. _____	bit	bitten
3. forget	forgot	_____
4. break	_____	broken
5. write	wrote	_____
6. _____	bled	bled
7. undo	_____	undone
8. spread	spread	_____
9. _____	felt	felt
10. give	gave	_____

Grammar Minutes · Grade 6 © 2009 Creative Teaching Press

Minute 22

Name _____

For Numbers 1–5, read each sentence, and underline the progressive verb phrase. Then circle the verb tense: *past progressive, present progressive,* or *future progressive.*
(Hint: Use the helping verb in each sentence to help you decide the tense.)

1. We are expecting a large crowd for the family reunion.

        past progressive   present progressive   future progressive

2. My cousins and their parents are staying at our house for a week.

        past progressive   present progressive   future progressive

3. Mom and Aunt Anna were planning the itinerary.

        past progressive   present progressive   future progressive

4. They will be entertaining many out-of-town guests.

        past progressive   present progressive   future progressive

5. Dad was encouraging me to organize a talent show for the children.

        past progressive   present progressive   future progressive

For Numbers 6–10, write the present progressive form to replace each underlined verb phrase.

6. I was thinking that a play of our family history would be a better idea. _____

7. Cousin Greg will be helping me write and direct it. _____

8. They will be creating the set and costumes. _____

9. Dad was saying how this is a good idea. _____

10. I will be looking forward to the festivities! _____

Progressive Verbs

Minute 23

Name _____

Read each sentence and underline the transitive verb. Then draw an arrow from the transitive verb to its object.
(**Hint**: A *transitive* verb is an action verb that requires the use of a direct object to answer *whom?* or *what?* Example: The judge <u>sentenced</u> the man to three years in prison.)

1. Tana loves her grandparents.

2. They know many things.

3. Grandpa collects coins.

4. He tells the history behind each one.

5. He also builds miniature sailboats.

6. On Sunday, he showed his latest masterpiece to Tana.

7. Grandma writes delightful poetry for children.

8. She sends her verses to all her children and grandchildren.

9. They enjoy reading them aloud to each other.

10. Tana memorizes her favorite rhymes.

Grammar Minutes · Grade 6 © 2009 Creative Teaching Press

Minute 24

Name _____

Read each sentence and underline the intransitive verb or verbs. If the sentence contains a boldfaced word or phrase, circle the question it answers about the verb: *how, where,* or *when.*

1. The hurricane winds blew **loud and fast**.

       how   where   when

2. Hannah hid **in the shower**.

       how   where   when

3. The trees creaked and moaned.

       how   where   when

4. Windows rattled.

       how   where   when

5. The rain fell **constantly** for five hours.

       how   where   when

6. The storm **finally** died.

       how   where   when

7. It ended **around noon**.

       how   where   when

8. Hannah went **outside**.

       how   where   when

9. She stepped **carefully** over debris.

       how   where   when

10. Hannah and her neighbors gathered **on the sidewalk**.

       how   where   when

Grammar Minutes · Grade 6 © 2009 Creative Teaching Press

Intransitive Verbs

Minute 25

Name _____

Circle the verb that correctly completes each sentence.

1. Tony (doesn't/don't) like chocolate cake.

2. However, our brothers and my mother (love/loves) it.

3. They always (order/orders) chocolate cake for dessert at restaurants.

4. Tony (ask/asks) for cheesecake with fruit.

5. He usually (do/does) not finish it, though.

6. Mama (eat/eats) the leftovers.

7. Dad, Lisa, and Mama (prefer/prefers) chocolate cake.

8. Mama says it isn't good to eat until you (is/are) stuffed.

9. Dad does not listen, and he (do/does) it anyway.

10. Mama just (shake/shakes) her head.

Grammar Minutes · Grade 6 © 2009 Creative Teaching Press

Minute 26

Name _____

Find all of the action verbs in the box. Write them on the lines below.

read	travel	be	bye	listen
poor	am	save	gather	breath
eat	best	breathe	full	were
student	think	recognize	dance	funny

1. _____   6. _____

2. _____   7. _____

3. _____   8. _____

4. _____   9. _____

5. _____   10. _____

Grammar Minutes · Grade 6 © 2009 Creative Teaching Press

Action Verbs Review

Minute 27

Name _____

Read each sentence and underline the verbs or verb phrases. Then circle the verb form for each sentence: *helping* or *linking*.

1. Chris became irritated with his disobedient dog.

    helping   linking

2. He was trying to teach it tricks.

    helping   linking

3. I was watching them.

    helping   linking

4. Boxer was unruly and hyper from the beginning.

    helping   linking

5. He was running away from Chris.

    helping   linking

6. Chris felt very frustrated.

    helping   linking

7. Boxer was more and more uncooperative.

    helping   linking

8. Both Chris and Boxer were hoping for a break.

    helping   linking

9. Chris and I were relaxing on the porch.

    helping   linking

10. Boxer was finally calm.

    helping   linking

Grammar Minutes · Grade 6 © 2009 Creative Teaching Press

Minute 28

Name _____

Write the correct verb or verb phrase to complete the table.

	Present	Past Perfect	Present Perfect	Future Perfect
1.	_____	had swum	have swum	will have swum
2.	crawl	_____	have crawled	will have crawled
3.	_____	had drunk	have drunk	will have drunk
4.	break	_____	have broken	will have broken
5.	grow	had grown	_____	will have grown
6.	walk	had walked	have walked	_____
7.	fall	_____	have fallen	will have fallen
8.	hit	had hit	_____	will have hit
9.	grab	had grabbed	have grabbed	_____
10.	crush	_____	have crushed	will have crushed

Verb Tenses Review

Minute 29

Name _____

Circle the verb form—*transitive* or *intransitive*—for each sentence below.

1.	Tom joined the theater arts club.	transitive	intransitive
2.	He acts quite well.	transitive	intransitive
3.	Tom's audition began shakily.	transitive	intransitive
4.	He got the lead role in the school play.	transitive	intransitive
5.	He memorized his lines in no time.	transitive	intransitive
6.	He practiced each scene.	transitive	intransitive
7.	They rehearsed every day.	transitive	intransitive
8.	The theater teacher directed the rehearsals.	transitive	intransitive
9.	Opening night went smoothly.	transitive	intransitive
10.	The audience cheered wildly.	transitive	intransitive

Grammar Minutes · Grade 6 © 2009 Creative Teaching Press

Minute 30

Name _____

Write the correct verb form to complete each sentence.

1. Tina and her sister _____ late on Saturday mornings.
sleep   sleeps

2. Her mother doesn't even _____ to wake them up.
try   tries

3. When Tina finally _____ up, she is grouchy.
get   gets

4. She _____ not a morning person.
is   are

5. Tina and her mother _____ breakfast quietly.
eat   eats

6. Tina _____ more cheerful and awake.
feel   feels

7. After breakfast, they _____ their day.
plan   plans

8. Tina _____ an idea.
have   has

9. Tina and her sister _____ to go to the amusement park.
want   wants

10. They _____ going to have a great time.
is   are

Subject and Verb Agreement Review

Minute 31

Name _____

Circle each adjective. Then draw an arrow from the adjective to the noun it describes. The number in parentheses at the end of the sentence tells how many examples you will find.

1. We took a trip to the spectacular zoo in San Diego. (1)

2. The sunny weather made for a beautiful day. (2)

3. The first animals we visited were the scaly reptiles. (2)

4. Then we saw giant elephants. (1)

5. Did you know that elephants are hairy? (1)

6. We walked into a warm hut filled with tropical plants. (2)

7. The hut housed loose hummingbirds. (1)

8. We watched the busy birds drink sugary nectar. (2)

9. The large cats are a favorite sight. (2)

10. I like to watch the playful cubs. (1)

Grammar Minutes · Grade 6 © 2009 Creative Teaching Press

Minute 32

Name _____

Write the comparative and superlative form for each adjective.
(**Hint:** Remember that some *comparative adjectives* are made by adding –*er*, while others are made by adding *more* in front of them. Some *superlative adjectives* are made by adding –*est*, while others are made by adding *most* in front of them.)

Adjective	Comparative Form	Superlative Form
Ex: bitter	more bitter	most bitter
1. funny	_____	_____
2. expensive	_____	_____
3. long	_____	_____
4. sick	_____	_____
5. small	_____	_____
6. quick	_____	_____
7. exciting	_____	_____
8. hot	_____	_____
9. colorful	_____	_____
10. pretty	_____	_____

Comparative and Superlative Adjectives

Minute 33

Name _____

Write the comparative and superlative forms for each irregular adjective.
(**Hint:** A few adjectives are considered irregular because they are written as entirely different words in the comparative and superlative forms.

Adjective	Comparative	Superlative
good	**1.** _____	**2.** _____
bad	**3.** _____	**4.** _____
far	**5.** _____	**6.** _____
much	**7.** _____	**8.** _____
little	**9.** _____	**10.** _____

Minute 34

Name _____

Rewrite each adjective as an adverb. Then write the adverb and the verb it modifies as a phrase.

(**Hint:** An *adverb* is a word that tells *how, when,* or *where* something happens.)

Adjective	Adverb	Verb	Adverbial Phrase
Ex: proud	proudly	stood	proudly stood
1. bold	_____	walked	_____
2. calm	_____	spoke	_____
3. excited	_____	shout	_____
4. nervous	_____	wait	_____
5. loud	_____	bark	_____
6. easy	_____	pass	_____
7. quick	_____	heals	_____
8. complete	_____	finishes	_____
9. busy	_____	prepares	_____
10. brave	_____	jumps	_____

Adverbs

Minute 35

Name _____

Circle the adverb in each sentence. Then draw an arrow from the adverb to the verb it modifies.
(**Hint:** An *adverb* is a word that tells *how, when,* or *where* something happens.)

1. Leah happily agreed to play tennis with her sister.

2. Andrea serves the ball fiercely.

3. The ball flies swiftly over the net.

4. Leah reacts speedily to meet the ball.

5. She soundly hits the ball with her racket.

6. Andrea barely misses the ball.

7. When it is Leah's turn to serve, she swings wildly.

8. Andrea returns the ball expertly.

9. The girls' skills are closely matched.

10. Andrea and Leah will gladly return to the tennis court.

Grammar Minutes · Grade 6 © 2009 Creative Teaching Press

Minute 36

Name _____

Circle the adverb in each sentence. Then draw an arrow from the adverb to the verb it modifies.
(**Hint:** An *adverb* is a word that tells *how, when,* or *where* something happens.)

1. Norberto always coaches a junior league baseball team.

2. The players are young, but they work hard to please him.

3. Melanie catches every ball that comes near her.

4. Out of everyone, Edwin runs the fastest.

5. Tucker hits the ball the farthest.

6. Norberto shouted often during the last game.

7. He pointed and yelled, "Throw the ball there!"

8. The ball buzzed close to the ground, but Melanie caught it.

9. Norberto's team won again.

10. "You have done well!" Norberto congratulated his players.

Adverbs without –ly

Minute 37

Name _____

Draw a line from each word to its synonym.

1.	damp	imitate
2.	avoid	ignore
3.	stop	grasp
4.	definite	faithful
5.	grab	angry
6.	copy	challenge
7.	loyal	moist
8.	furious	discontinue
9.	dare	perplex
10.	baffle	certain

Grammar Minutes · Grade 6 © 2009 Creative Teaching Press

Minute 38

Name _____

Draw a line from each word to its antonym.

1.	drenched	busy
2.	bright	dead
3.	seize	dull
4.	alive	awake
5.	complex	simple
6.	hefty	smooth
7.	seldom	give
8.	asleep	dry
9.	coarse	often
10.	idle	light

Antonyms

Minute 39

Name _____

Write a homophone for each word.
(**Hint:** *Homophones* sound the same but mean different things and are spelled differently.)

1. right _____

2. through _____

3. here _____

4. meet _____

5. seam _____

6. hair _____

7. bear _____

8. dear _____

9. steel _____

10. roll _____

Grammar Minutes · Grade 6 © 2009 Creative Teaching Press

Minute 40

Name _____

For Numbers 1–3, circle the word that correctly completes each sentence.

1. An adjective modifies a (noun, verb).

2. A (comparative, superlative) adjective compares or contrasts two things.

3. A (comparative, superlative) adjective compares or contrasts three or more things.

For Numbers 4–10, write the adjectives from the box that correctly complete the paragraph. Use each adjective only once.

> helpful   better   undefeated   quick   shaky   advanced   winning

Rose is a _____ soccer player than I am. She has _____ reflexes.
                    4.   5.
Unfortunately, at first my passing skills were _____. However, Rose is a _____
                                                          6.   7.
coach. I am a more _____ player since she has worked with me. I even scored
                              8.
the _____ goal at our last game. Our team is now _____ .
          9.   10.

4. _____   **8.** _____

5. _____   **9.** _____

6. _____   **10.** _____

7. _____

Adjectives Review

Minute 41

Name _____

For Numbers 1–5, circle the correct comparative or superlative adjective to complete each sentence.

1. Janelle is the (shorter/more shorter) of the two girls.

2. After two days of being sick, Matthew felt (worse/more bad) than ever.

3. Brian and Jason have curly hair, but Fred's is the (curliest/most curliest).

4. She felt (more lonelier/lonelier) at night during her week at camp.

5. This stationery has (cuter/more cute) designs.

For Numbers 6–10, write the comparative and superlative forms of each adjective.

Adjective	Comparative Form	Superlative Form
6. big	_____	_____
7. little	_____	_____
8. much	_____	_____
9. sleepy	_____	_____
10. good	_____	_____

Grammar Minutes · Grade 6 © 2009 Creative Teaching Press

Minute 42

Name _____

Circle the adverb in each sentence. Then draw an arrow from the adverb to the verb or verb phrase it modifies.

1. Ted and Mario always go camping in March.

2. It usually rains in April.

3. "Let's pitch our tent here," Ted said.

4. "No, let's camp closer to the creek," Mario answered.

5. They waited patiently for their dinner.

6. Mario deftly cleaned the fish.

7. Ted carefully lit a fire to cook them.

8. They ate happily and then went to sleep.

9. In the morning, they hiked up the mountain cautiously.

10. They leisurely admired the view from the top.

Grammar Minutes · Grade 6 © 2009 Creative Teaching Press

Adverbs Review

Minute 43

Name _____

Read each pair of words. Write *S* if they are synonyms or *A* if they are antonyms.

1. loyal, devoted   _____

2. alive, dead   _____

3. imitate, mimic   _____

4. constantly, never   _____

5. identical, unlike   _____

6. complex, straightforward   _____

7. avoid, ignore   _____

8. halt, cease   _____

9. humorous, comical   _____

10. relaxed, tense   _____

Grammar Minutes · Grade 6 © 2009 Creative Teaching Press

Minute 44

Name _____

Write the correct homophone from the box to complete each sentence.

to/too/two	sea/see	flour/flower
your/you're	there/they're/their	needed/kneaded
weather/whether	pale/pail	wood/would
piece/peace		

1. The child took his shovel and his _____ to the beach to build sandcastles.

2. The _____ was sunny and perfect.

3. The family ate a picnic lunch right _____ on the beach.

4. The seagulls wanted some lunch, _____ .

5. He pretended to make bread and added _____ to his mixture.

6. He _____ the pretend dough.

7. "Would you like a _____ of bread?" he asked.

8. "I _____ ," replied his mother.

9. "Seth, _____ a good baker!" she said.

10. They pretended to eat, and then they swam in the _____.

Homophones Review

Minute 45

Name _____

Circle the correct conjunction to complete each sentence.
(**Hint**: A *conjunction* is a word that joins words or groups of words. It can show togetherness or contrast.)

1. Rafael wanted to join the football team; (however/since/or), his mother thought it was too dangerous.

2. He borrowed his friend's uniform (and/so/because) she could see the protective gear he would wear.

3. Rafael (yet/or/and) Dad convinced his mother to go to a practice.

4. They knew it could help change her mind, (because/or/and) it might convince her she's right.

5. Rafael's mother saw that the boys played hard, (although/but/also) the coaches supervised them well.

6. She said Rafael could join the team, (since/except/because) he had to promise to be careful.

7. Rafael didn't know whether to jump for joy (but/and/or) nod seriously.

8. Rafael's mother had relented, (because/or/yet) she was still worried about his safety.

9. Rafael is an excellent defender, (so/or/because) he made the team.

10. Rafael's mother (but/yet/and) father went to every game.

Grammar Minutes · Grade 6 © 2009 Creative Teaching Press

Minute 46

Name _____

For each sentence, underline the compound subject. If a sentence does not have a compound subject, write *None* on the line.
(**Hint:** A *compound subject* has two or more simple subjects with the same predicate.)

1. Annie visits Sandy's Ice-Cream Shop every Friday.   _____

2. She and her friends love to go there after school.   _____

3. Lemon custard and butter pecan are her two
   favorite flavors.   _____

4. Chocolate sprinkles, walnuts, or chocolate chips
   make great toppings.   _____

5. Annie likes them both.   _____

6. She orders something different each time she
   goes there.   _____

7. Sandy lets Annie sample new flavors and new
   toppings before ordering them.   _____

8. Sundaes and milkshakes are also popular treats.   _____

9. Annie and Sandy have become friends.   _____

10. Sandy told Annie she could work at the ice-cream
    shop when she is old enough.   _____

Compound Subjects

Minute 47

Name _____

For each sentence, circle the compound predicate's verbs. If a sentence does not have compound predicate verbs, write *None* on the line.

1. Jenny tumbles and dives competitively. _____

2. She dreams of competing at the Olympics and believes one day she will. _____

3. She trains very hard at both sports. _____

4. Jenny thinks hard and ponders which sport to stick with. _____

5. Her training sessions are long and hard. _____

6. Jenny and her mother feel she can't possibly keep doing both. _____

7. Jenny's schoolwork gets more difficult each year. _____

8. Her coaches have been supportive and have worked around her schedule. _____

9. Jenny's parents are not rushing her decision. _____

10. They encourage her and tell her to take her time. _____

Grammar Minutes · Grade 6 © 2009 Creative Teaching Press

Minute 48

Name _____

For Numbers 1–5, circle the preposition in each group of words.

1. red   before   earlier

2. after   previously   stay

3. during   quietly   very

4. near   set   yesterday

5. to   how   two

For Numbers 6–10, circle the prepositional phrase in each sentence.

6. The cat spotted a squirrel in the yard and decided to try to catch it.

7. It chased the squirrel across the grass.

8. They ran between the houses where I could barely see them.

9. The speedy squirrel escaped into the alley.

10. It turned the corner, ran up a telephone pole, and disappeared.

Grammar Minutes · Grade 6 © 2009 Creative Teaching Press

Minute 49

Name _____

For Numbers 1–5, circle the five dependent clauses in the box.
(**Hint**: A *dependent clause* does not express a complete thought and is not a complete sentence on its own.)

> when the cake was served
>
> she came home at last
>
> if you need my opinion
>
> because I was tired
>
> that slobbery dog pants
>
> and if I remember correctly
>
> until the police arrived

For Numbers 6–10, underline the dependent clause in each sentence.

6. My friend, who does not have a dog, loves to play with mine.

7. I don't know what happened yesterday.

8. Wherever Mason goes, he is loved.

9. If you agree to help, I won't forget it.

10. The cat that has the white patches is mine.

Grammar Minutes · Grade 6 © 2009 Creative Teaching Press

Minute 50

Name _____

For Numbers 1–5, circle the five independent clauses in the box.
(**Hint**: An *independent clause* expresses a complete thought and could stand alone as its own sentence.)

after supper

I know Mr. Fletcher

because she was ill

Maria is a letter carrier

please pass the potatoes

the sun came up

carry the boxes

For Numbers 6–10, underline the independent clause in each sentence.

6. Thomas is a veterinarian who makes house calls.

7. They care for animals more than most people.

8. With skilled expertise, they help sick pets.

9. People count on them to make their animals well.

10. I want to be like them when I grow up.

Minute 51

Name _____

Insert the missing commas in each sentence.

1. Even though Ralph and Linda are siblings they get along pretty well.

2. Their television preferences differ so they try to compromise when deciding what to watch.

3. Ralph likes to watch comedies talk shows and action shows but Linda likes dramas detective shows and game shows.

4. Sometimes they argue but the fight never lasts long.

5. Their parents usually don't have to get involved although that used to happen a lot.

6. They would shout at each other and they were so loud the neighbors could hear them.

7. This embarrassed their parents so they taught Ralph and Linda how to be cooperative with one another.

8. Ralph and Linda composed a schedule of who gets to decide what to watch and it worked.

9. They based the schedule on favorite shows but each person ended up having to sacrifice one or two shows.

10. Their parents were happy and the neighbors were relieved.

Grammar Minutes · Grade 6 © 2009 Creative Teaching Press

Minute 52

Name _____

For each sentence, write *Yes* if it is a compound sentence or *No* if it is not.
(**Hint:** A *compound sentence* has more than one independent clause, which are often joined by a conjunction.)

1. Katy's vacation to Hawaii was splendid. _____

2. She took tours of Oahu, Maui, and Kauai. _____

3. Visiting three islands was exhausting, but she loved every minute of it. _____

4. The favorite part of her trip was swimming with dolphins. _____

5. The gentle creatures snickered, and they seemed to invite her to play. _____

6. The marine biologist taught the visitors about dolphin behavior, so Katy listened carefully. _____

7. Dolphins are very intelligent, social creatures. _____

8. Katy did not see any hair on the dolphins, so she was surprised to learn they are mammals. _____

9. The dolphins easily entertained the crowd, and the dolphins looked happy as well. _____

10. Katy is thinking she might like to become a marine biologist one day. _____

Compound Sentences

Minute 53

Name _____

For each sentence, write *Yes* if it is a complex sentence or *No* if it is not.
(**Hint:** A *complex sentence* combines an independent clause with one or more dependent clauses.)

1. My sister's hamster was very sick. _____

2. When I saw how sad Andrea was, I wanted to help. _____

3. I took Minnie to the veterinarian, even though I don't like hamsters. _____

4. After examining Minnie, Dr. Rains gave her some medicine. _____

5. Dr. Rains gave me more medicine to take home for Minnie. _____

6. I gave Minnie the medicine because Andrea couldn't administer it properly. _____

7. Before we knew it, she was running on her exercise wheel. _____

8. When Minnie began to perk up, Andrea perked up, too. _____

9. She made a thank-you card for me. _____

10. It made me happy, and I was glad that I helped. _____

Grammar Minutes · Grade 6 © 2009 Creative Teaching Press

Minute 54

Name _____

Underline both independent clauses in each compound-complex sentence.

1. Giovanna joined the marching band, but Selma, who was more athletic, joined the basketball team.

2. Giovanna thought that Selma was making a mistake, but Selma, who is usually indecisive, was sure of her decision.

3. The girls were sad not to be in the same classes, but they both looked forward to new experiences because they spent all their time together.

4. Since the school year started, the girls barely saw each other, and they missed their close friendship.

5. They got together on weekends, and they talked about everything that came to mind.

6. Giovanna and Selma supported each other, but they didn't agree about all things, like which extra-curricular activity to join.

7. Even though the girls didn't see each other often, they remained friends and they introduced one another to new people.

8. Giovanna and Selma were both hard workers, and they excelled at their talents, which made their parents proud.

9. Giovanna, who had joined the drum section, played the cadence at Selma's basketball games, and the crowd loved it.

10. The cadence sparked energy in the team, so they played better when the drum section was there.

Grammar Minutes · Grade 6 © 2009 Creative Teaching Press

Compound-Complex Sentences

Minute 55

Name _____

For Numbers 1–5, write five conjunctions from the box on the lines below.

| always | but | because | very | so | however | yours | and | up |

1. _____

2. _____

3. _____

4. _____

5. _____

For Numbers 6–10, circle the conjunction in each sentence.

6. Matthew wanted to be an astronaut, but he had poor math skills.

7. He had to do something or he would fall too far behind in class to catch up.

8. His mother took him to a tutor so Matthew would get more individual instruction.

9. Matthew's tutor was firm, yet he was very helpful.

10. Matthew's grades began to improve, and his confidence soared.

Grammar Minutes · Grade 6 © 2009 Creative Teaching Press

Minute 56

Name _____

Circle either *compound subject* or *compound predicate* to describe each sentence.
(**Hint**: A *compound subject* has two or more simple subjects with the same predicate.
A *compound predicate* has two or more predicates sharing the same subject.)

1. Hawaii was built by volcanoes and still continues to grow through volcanic activity.

    compound subject   compound predicate

2. Hawaii became a state in 1959 and is a lovely vacation spot.

    compound subject   compound predicate

3. Culture and traditions are very important to native Hawaiian people.

    compound subject   compound predicate

4. Vacationers are greeted with "Aloha!" and receive flower leis.

    compound subject   compound predicate

5. Kauai and Maui are popular islands to visit.

    compound subject   compound predicate

6. Honolulu is densely populated and serves as the islands' capital city.

    compound subject   compound predicate

7. Citizens of Hawaii and many visitors fight to preserve the natural beauty of the islands.

    compound subject   compound predicate

8. Endangered sea turtles and other marine life swim free in Hawaii's waters.

    compound subject   compound predicate

9. Lava erupts from Kilauea Volcano and flows to the sea.

    compound subject   compound predicate

10. The beautiful scenery and gentle weather make for a balmy paradise.

    compound subject   compound predicate

Grammar Minutes · Grade 6 © 2009 Creative Teaching Press
Compound Subjects and Compound Predicates Review

Minute 57

Name _____

For Numbers 1–5, write the correct preposition from the box to complete each sentence. Use each preposition only once.

> inside   behind   before   near   after

1. It's never a good idea to hide _____ a car.

2. It's not a good idea to swim right _____ you eat.

3. Children should never play _____ an open flame.

4. Never leave your pet _____ a hot car.

5. Always look both ways _____ crossing the street.

For Numbers 6–10, write your own prepositional phrase to complete each sentence.

6. The children walked _____.

7. Their playhouse was located _____.

8. Two girls leaned _____.

9. They talked _____.

10. They felt safe _____.

Grammar Minutes · Grade 6 © 2009 Creative Teaching Press

Minute 58

Name _____

Circle either *dependent clause* or *independent clause* to describe the underlined words in each sentence.

1.	Alaska entered the Union in 1959 <u>as the 49th state</u>.	dependent clause	independent clause
2.	Alaska is separated from the United States by Canada, <u>and it is more than twice the size of Texas</u>.	dependent clause	independent clause
3.	<u>Juneau is Alaska's state capital</u>, but Anchorage is the most populous city.	dependent clause	independent clause
4.	<u>If you would like to visit Juneau</u>, you would have to fly on an airplane.	dependent clause	independent clause
5.	<u>Alaska has many islands</u>, so it has many miles of shoreline.	dependent clause	independent clause
6.	In summer, daytime temperatures range from 60° to 90° F, <u>so they vary greatly</u>.	dependent clause	independent clause
7.	<u>If you visit Anchorage in the fall</u>, you might see the northern lights.	dependent clause	independent clause
8.	The average winter temperature there is about 15°F <u>so you would have to bundle up!</u>	dependent clause	independent clause
9.	<u>Alaska is home to Mount McKinley</u>, the highest point in North America.	dependent clause	independent clause
10.	Sled dogs, <u>which are often mixed breeds</u>, pull heavy loads and people through harsh climates.	dependent clause	independent clause

Grammar Minutes · Grade 6 © 2009 Creative Teaching Press

Dependent and Independent Clauses Review

Minute 59

Name _____

For Numbers 1–5, write *dependent clause(s)* or *independent clause(s)* to correctly complete each sentence.

1. A compound sentence joins two _____ .

2–3. A complex sentence has one _____ and one

or more _____ .

4–5. A compound-complex sentence joins two or more _____

and one or more _____ .

For Numbers 6–10, read each sentence, and circle whether it is *compound,* *complex,* or *compound-complex.*

6. Gymnastics is a difficult sport, and it requires excellent coordination and balance.

    a. compound   **b.** complex   **c.** compound-complex

7. The apparatuses on which gymnasts compete are different for men than they are for women.

    a. compound   **b.** complex   **c.** compound-complex

8. Both men and women do the floor and vault exercises, but all the other events are different.

    a. compound   **b.** complex   **c.** compound-complex

9. The balance beam, which Rena thinks is the most difficult apparatus, is four inches wide, and it stands four feet and one inch high.

    a. compound   **b.** complex   **c.** compound-complex

10. Tom finds the pommel horse most challenging, so he trains very hard to improve his skills on it.

    a. compound   **b.** complex   **c.** compound-complex

Grammar Minutes · Grade 6 © 2009 Creative Teaching Press

Minute 60

Name _____

Circle the appositive phrase in each sentence.
(**Hint:** An *appositive* identifies or renames the words before it. Example: Our teachers, *Mr. Jones and Ms. Liddell,* went to a conference on Friday.)

1. Mount Everest, the mountain with the highest altitude in the world, is located in the Himalayan Mountain Range.

2. Mount Everest is about 29,029 feet, or 8,848 meters, above sea level.

3. Edmund Hillary, one of the first men to climb Mount Everest, received knighthood for his spectacular achievement.

4. Junko Tabei, a Japanese mountain climber, was the first woman to scale Mount Everest.

5. Summiting, or reaching the top of a mountain, gives mountain climbers a tremendous sense of satisfaction.

6. Avalanches cause most of the fatalities, or deaths, among mountain climbers on Mount Everest.

7. Mauna Kea, an inactive volcano in Hawaii, is actually taller than Mount Everest when the portion below sea level is included in the measurement.

8. K2, the second highest mountain on earth, measures 28,251 feet above sea level.

9. The mountain in North America that has the highest peak above sea level, Mount McKinley, is located in Alaska.

10. Mount McKinley is 20,320 feet, or 6,193.6 meters, above sea level.

Appositives

Minute 61

Name _____

For each sentence, insert the missing commas in the correct places.

1. Ren's birthday is June 15 1996.

2. He wants to eat pizza go bowling and open presents on his birthday.

3. On his last birthday he had a swimming party.

4. It had been a hot humid day.

5. You were at Ren's party weren't you?

6. Ren's father said "Ren you remember to thank your guests for coming."

7. Ren answered "Don't worry Dad!"

8. Ren wishes to go to Anaheim California on his birthday.

9. He says "Celebrating at Disneyland would be great fun!"

10. For now he will be content with sticking close to home.

Grammar Minutes · Grade 6 © 2009 Creative Teaching Press

Minute 62

Name _____

Insert the missing quotation marks for each sentence. If the sentence does not need quotation marks, write *None* on the line.

1. Have you ever seen a manatee? I asked Don. _____

2. He said that he had not. _____

3. I told him that they were large marine mammals that are shaped like seals. _____

4. Oh! he exclaimed. I have read about them. _____

5. Don't they live in waters off the coast of Texas and Florida? he asked. _____

6. Yes, but manatees are endangered, I answered. _____

7. Don informed me that many weigh over 1,000 pounds. _____

8. I read that they are sometimes called sea cows, Don added. _____

9. Ben lives in Florida, and he sees them sometimes, I said. _____

10. What other marine life is endangered? Don asked. _____

Minute 63

Name _____

Circle the two words in each sentence that can be combined to form a contraction. Write the contraction on the line.

1. Earlier they were out, but they are at home now. _____

2. Mr. Hoff told him that he should have studied more. _____

3. You will be disappointed. _____

4. It is almost the holidays! _____

5. Either I can pick up the food or we will dine in. _____

6. On vacation days, they would take the train to the beach. _____

7. She does not have a train pass. _____

8. "Do not leave without me!" _____

9. Peonies and tulips are not in season. _____

10. You have finished already? _____

Grammar Minutes · Grade 6 © 2009 Creative Teaching Press

Minute 64

Name _____

For each sentence, circle the title or address word and write its abbreviation on the line.

1. I shop at Mister Gregorino's store. _____

2. Missus Gregorino, his mother, opened the store in 1924. _____

3. The store will be passed on to George Gregorino Junior when he is ready. _____

4. They asked Senator Miller to give them advice. _____

5. I need to see my dermatologist, Doctor Sykes, for this rash. _____

6. Captain Pullman stood on deck surveying the ocean. _____

7. I used to live by Marty's Dry Cleaners on Sixth Avenue. _____

8. The cross street for Marty's is 36th Street. _____

9. Take a left onto Linden Boulevard. _____

10. Highway 57 has an on-ramp on the right side of the street. _____

Abbreviations

Minute 65

Name _____

For each sentence, insert the missing semicolon in the correct place.

1. Seth and Victor were in an accident however, they were not injured.

2. Jesse was the only actor who memorized the lines therefore, he got the lead role.

3. I should not have slipped then I might have won the race.

4. Kory got bucked off his horse however, he got right back on.

5. My dog, Matilda, loves to ride in the car therefore, I take her everywhere dogs are allowed.

6. Janice thought the critics were wrong to criticize her play indeed, they simply did not understand it.

7. Martine didn't think anyone noticed her mistake besides, she didn't care if they did.

8. Buddy was an excellent teacher however, his students thought he was strict.

9. Tiffany learned to drive on a deserted old ranch road indeed, it had been located in the middle of nowhere.

10. Rhode Island is the smallest state in the United States however, it has the longest official name: "State of Rhode Island and the Providence Plantations."

Grammar Minutes · Grade 6 © 2009 Creative Teaching Press

Minute 66

Name _____

For Numbers 1–3, write a word from the box to correctly complete each sentence.

> closing   dialogue   appositive   greeting   list   action

1. In a business letter, a colon is placed after the _____ .

2. A colon used after the sentence *Use the following ingredients* signals a _____ .

3. In plays, colons follow names to signal _____ .

For Numbers 4–10, insert the missing colon in the correct place.

4. The bread recipe calls for four ingredients yeast, water, flour, and salt.

5. Jason Hi Kathleen! I've been looking for you everywhere.

6. Let me make the following suggestions first, take notes; second, ask questions; and third, review your notes after the lecture.

7. Dear Sir We met at the Mytown Chamber of Commerce Meeting last week.

8. Please bring the following supplies scissors, glue, map, pencils, and an eraser.

9. To Whom It May Concern I am writing in response to the job advertisement in *The Chronicle*.

10. Send the check to the following address 227 Montgomery Ave.

Colons

Minute 67

Name _____

Write *sit* or *set* to complete each sentence.

1. Please _____ your drink on the coaster.

2. Come _____ and talk with me for a while.

3. The sun has always _____ to the west.

4. Daisy _____ the books on the table.

5. My dog has not yet learned to _____ .

6. My grandmother does not like to _____ for long periods of time.

7. Mother asked her to _____ the table for dinner.

8. We _____ at the table to eat dinner.

9. _____ the groceries on the counter before you drop the bags!

10. The vase will be _____ on the mantle to decorate the room.

Grammar Minutes · Grade 6 © 2009 Creative Teaching Press

Minute 68

Name _____

Write *lie* or *lay* to complete each sentence.

1. I will _____ my cards on the table for you.

2. I asked if I could _____ down in the nurse's office.

3. Don't _____ the matches where they will get damp.

4. Will you _____ the baby in his crib?

5. The child was sick and could do nothing but _____ in bed.

6. When I feel lazy, I just _____ on the couch and watch television.

7. What does it feel like to _____ on a water bed?

8. I will _____ the mail on the desk for you.

9. My dogs Shaggy and Trevor _____ in the sun.

10. I _____ my bag on the chair.

Word Usage: Lie or Lay

Minute 69

Name _____

Write *your* or *you're* to complete each sentence.

1. I hope _____ going to come to the party.

2. _____ parents said they would pick you up at 8 o'clock.

3. They will use _____ brother's car.

4. Bring _____ favorite music to the party.

5. _____ a great singer.

6. _____ friends would love to hear you sing a song.

7. Do _____ nerves bother you when you perform?

8. What do you do while _____ waiting to go on stage?

9. All of _____ hard work and constant practicing has paid off.

10. I'll be sure that _____ singing at my next party.

Minute 70

Name _____

Underline the appositive phrase in each sentence.
(**Hint:** Check the remaining words—they should still form a sentence that makes sense.)

1. Austin, the capital of Texas, is centrally located.

2. Washington, D.C., the capital of the United States, is a great place to visit.

3. Delaware, the first state to ratify the U.S. Constitution, is nicknamed the Diamond State.

4. Georgia, the Peach State, was one of the original thirteen colonies founded on American soil.

5. Juneau, Alaska's capital city, is the most remotely located capital city in the United States.

6. The state capital of Florida, the Sunshine State, is Tallahassee.

7. Lansing is the capital of Michigan, the Great Lakes State.

8. The capital of Connecticut, the Constitution State, is Hartford.

9. The Statue of Liberty is located in New York, the Empire State.

10. Many years ago, people rushed to California, now called the Golden State, to look for gold.

Appositives Review

Minute 71

Name _____

Insert commas and quotation marks in the correct places to complete each sentence.

1. What type of books do you like to read? Mrs. Turner asked me.

2. I like to read mysteries historical fiction and poetry I replied.

3. She said that I could borrow her books and she helped me choose the first one.

4. It was a fictional story about a girl who lived in Atlanta Georgia during the Civil War.

5. When I was finished with it I asked Mrs. Turner May I borrow another?

6. She replied Of course you may.

7. Carlie you should keep a journal and write notes about all the books you read Mrs. Turner suggested.

8. I wrote in a journal every night and soon I began to have ideas about stories I could write.

9. The more I wrote the stronger my writing became.

10. I enjoy reading and writing more than ever now thanks to Mrs. Turner.

Grammar Minutes · Grade 6 © 2009 Creative Teaching Press

Minute 72

Name _____

For Numbers 1–5, underline the two words in each sentence that can be combined to form a contraction. Write the contraction on the line.

1. We are ready to leave school. _____

2. Raise your hand if you are going on the bus today. _____

3. Although the weatherman said it was going to be cold, it is sunny and warm. _____

4. She could have had two cookies, but she only took one. _____

5. Laura and I said that we would go to the store to pick up the milk. _____

For Numbers 6–10, write the full word for each abbreviation.

6. Capt. _____

7. Sen. _____

8. Blvd. _____

9. Mr. _____

10. Hwy. _____

Grammar Minutes · Grade 6 © 2009 Creative Teaching Press

Contractions and Abbreviations Review

Minute 73

Name _____

For Numbers 1–5, write *C* for colon or *S* for semicolon to tell what punctuation mark should be used in each example.

1. After the greeting in a business letter _____

2. To set off a list of items _____

3. To join two independent clauses _____

4. Before words such as *therefore, however,* and *besides* _____

5. Instead of a period to introduce a series of related sentences _____

For Numbers 6–10, insert either a colon or a semicolon in each sentence.

6. I should have worked late then I would have finished the project.

7. I need these things from the grocery store eggs, milk, butter, and yogurt.

8. Please send the package to this address 1999 Hummingbird Lane.

9. Leila was the only brave one therefore, they all followed her lead.

10. Follow these steps first, glue the pom-pom onto the craft sticks; second, secure the pipe cleaners in place; third, add the stickers for eyes.

Grammar Minutes · Grade 6 © 2009 Creative Teaching Press

Minute 74

Name _____

Circle the word that best completes each sentence.

1. _____ desk is always neater than mine.
    Your   You're

2. Your pencils _____ neatly in your pencil box.
    lie   lay

3. You always _____ your books in your desk in a tidy stack.
    sit   set

4. _____ always prepared because your supplies are organized.
    Your   You're

5. Maybe if I _____ next to you, I will learn better organizational skills.
    sit   set

6. It's frustrating to never know where I have _____ my things.
    sit   set

7. Will you help me organize my desk like _____ desk?
    your   you're

8. You can _____ back and relax on that couch while you tell me what
    lie   lay
    to do.

9. _____ a helpful person.
    Your   You're

10. When I _____ down to sleep tonight, I will give thanks that you
    lie   lay
    helped me.

Word Usage Review

Minute 75

Name _____

Circle the interjection in each sentence.

1. Hey! Give that back.

2. Oops! I forgot my homework.

3. Oh, look at that cute puppy!

4. Help! I've fallen and I can't get up!

5. We won the game! Hooray!

6. I bumped my funny bone. Ouch! That really hurts!

7. Well, better luck next time.

8. I spilled the milk. Oh, no! Can you help me wipe it up?

9. Whoa! That was a close call!

10. Mom said I can't go. Rats! Maybe next time.

Grammar Minutes · Grade 6 © 2009 Creative Teaching Press

Minute 76

Name _____

Complete each sentence with the correct article: *a, an,* or *the.*

1. Every day after school, I go with Mom to get _____ baby from daycare.

2. Then some days we go to the grocery store with _____ list of items we need.

3. "Please go get _____ fruit, while I get the other stuff," Mom says.

4. At the checkout stand, we realize we forgot _____ milk.

5. I hurry to the back of the store to grab _____ gallon of skim milk.

6. Sometimes I need a snack, so I'll eat _____ apple on the way home.

7. Every Friday, Mom starts to prepare lasagna as soon as we get home. It makes _____ irresistible meal.

8. Morgan, _____ baby, is not old enough to enjoy it yet.

9. Mom sometimes feeds her _____ jar of mashed carrots.

10. Her face is _____ amusing sight when it's smeared with sticky, orange food.

Grammar Minutes · Grade 6 © 2009 Creative Teaching Press

Articles

Minute 77

Name _____

Add a prefix from the box to change the meaning of the word. You may use a prefix more than once.

| dis | un | ir | retro | anti | micro | non | multi |

Base Word	Prefix	New Word
1. assemble	_____	_____
2. sense	_____	_____
3. active	_____	_____
4. attractive	_____	_____
5. cultural	_____	_____
6. wave	_____	_____
7. reversible	_____	_____
8. dairy	_____	_____
9. bacterial	_____	_____
10. certain	_____	_____

Grammar Minutes · Grade 6 © 2009 Creative Teaching Press

Minute 78

Name _____

Rewrite each base word with the given suffix.
(**Hint:** Watch out for spelling changes!)

	Base Word	Suffix	New Word
1.	kind	-ness	_____
2.	happy	-ness	_____
3.	weary	-ness	_____
4.	soft	-ness	_____
5.	empty	-ness	_____
6.	intend	-tion	_____
7.	attend	-tion	_____
8.	subtract	-tion	_____
9.	elect	-tion	_____
10.	create	-tion	_____

Grammar Minutes · Grade 6 © 2009 Creative Teaching Press

Suffixes

Minute 79

Name _____

Rewrite each base word with the given prefix. You may use a prefix more than once.

| in | semi | im | auto | re | pre | de |

	Base Word	Prefix	New Word
1.	direct	_____	_____
2.	test	_____	_____
3.	appear	_____	_____
4.	circle	_____	_____
5.	graph	_____	_____
6.	form	_____	_____
7.	mobile	_____	_____
8.	caution	_____	_____
9.	possible	_____	_____
10.	decisive	_____	_____

Grammar Minutes · Grade 6 © 2009 Creative Teaching Press

Minute 80

Name _____

Rewrite each base word with the given suffix.
(**Hint:** Watch out for spelling changes!)

	Base Word	Suffix	New Word
1.	fold	-able	_____
2.	wash	-able	_____
3.	erase	-able	_____
4.	move	-able	_____
5.	like	-able	_____
6.	hope	-less	_____
7.	fear	-less	_____
8.	sense	-less	_____
9.	friend	-less	_____
10.	care	-less	_____

Grammar Minutes · Grade 6 © 2009 Creative Teaching Press

More Suffixes

Minute 81

Name _____

Draw a line from the Greek root word to its meaning. Draw another line from the meaning to the sample word.

	Root Word	Meaning	English Word
1.	dia	distance	podiatrist
2.	pod	time	metric
3.	chrono	foot	epidermis
4.	gen	skin	bibliography
5.	hydro	water	chronology
6.	tele	book	hydrate
7.	meter	life	telescope
8.	biblio	through or across	diagonal
9.	bio	measure	generation
10.	derm	birth	biology

Grammar Minutes · Grade 6 © 2009 Creative Teaching Press

Minute 82

Name _____

Draw a line from the Latin root word to its meaning. Draw another line from the meaning to the sample word.

	Root Word	Meaning	English Word
1.	sol	plant	aquarium
2.	aqua	right	affix
3.	cred	write	inscribe
4.	herb	water	pedicure
5.	pedi	sun	territory
6.	terra	fasten	incredible
7.	fix	belief	construct
8.	scrib	build	justice
9.	just	feet	solar
10.	struct	earth	herbivore

Grammar Minutes • Grade 6 © 2009 Creative Teaching Press

Latin Root Words

Minute 83

Name _____

Write *C* for each word if it is spelled correctly. If the word is spelled incorrectly, write the correct spelling on the line.

1. friend _____

2. recieve _____

3. sieze _____

4. beleive _____

5. neighbor _____

6. retreive _____

7. either _____

8. wierd _____

9. eerie _____

10. field _____

Grammar Minutes · Grade 6 © 2009 Creative Teaching Press

Minute 84

Name _____

Write C for each word if it is spelled correctly. If the word is spelled incorrectly, write the correct spelling on the line.

1. monkies _____

2. flies _____

3. ladies _____

4. babies _____

5. fries _____

6. turkies _____

7. holidays _____

8. cries _____

9. chimnies _____

10. journies _____

Grammar Minutes • Grade 6 © 2009 Creative Teaching Press

More Spelling Patterns and Exceptions

Minute 85

Name _____

For Numbers 1–5, write the words that signal negatives.

no	barely	always	nowhere	everywhere
either	nobody	any	all	neither

1. _____

2. _____

3. _____

4. _____

5. _____

For Numbers 6–10, write *C* next to the sentence if it uses the negatives correctly. If the sentence uses the negative incorrectly, write *I*.

6. I didn't buy no Halloween candy for trick-or-treaters yet. _____

7. My brother does not want to wear a costume this year. _____

8. I can't barely wait to wear my ghoulish costume! _____

9. My little sister doesn't like it none. _____

10. Nobody helped me make the costume. _____

Grammar Minutes · Grade 6 © 2009 Creative Teaching Press

Minute 86

Name _____

For Numbers 1–5, write an interjection before each sentence.

1. _____! Do you have the time?

2. _____! I sprained my ankle!

3. _____, we will do better next time.

4. _____! I left my grocery list at home.

5. _____, what an adorable creature!

For Numbers 6–10, write the correct article, *a, an,* or *the,* before each group of words.

6. _____ Lincoln Memorial

7. _____ piece of paper

8. _____ hour and a half

9. _____ last person in that line

10. _____ ant farm

Grammar Minutes · Grade 6 © 2009 Creative Teaching Press

Interjections and Articles Review

Minute 87

Name _____

Write the meaning of each word using the prefix to help you.

1. nontoxic _____

2. inflexible _____

3. autobiography _____

4. microchip _____

5. disconnect _____

6. preview _____

7. dishonest _____

8. multiuse _____

9. semiannual _____

10. impossible _____

Grammar Minutes · Grade 6 © 2009 Creative Teaching Press

Minute 88

Name _____

Add a suffix from the box to each root word to create a new word.

-some	-ness	-tion	-less	-able

1. dark _____

2. fascinate _____

3. narrate _____

4. thought _____

5. worthy _____

6. restless _____

7. comfort _____

8. sense _____

9. weary _____

10. agree _____

Grammar Minutes · Grade 6 © 2009 Creative Teaching Press

Suffixes Review

Minute 89

Name _____

Draw a line from the Greek or Latin root word to its meaning.

1. pod   far away

2. chrono   time

3. tele   write

4. bio   life

5. derm   build

6. struct   sun

7. scrib   skin

8. sol   right

9. terra   foot

10. just   earth

Minute 90

Name _____

For Numbers 1–5, cross out the word that is spelled incorrectly.

1. **a.** relieve   **b.** cieling   **c.** brief

2. **a.** conceit   **b.** vein   **c.** frieght

3. **a.** mischief   **b.** peirce   **c.** neither

4. **a.** sieze   **b.** cashier   **c.** deceive

5. **a.** conceive   **b.** nieghbor   **c.** weird

For Numbers 6–10, write *C* if the word is spelled correctly. If the word is spelled incorrectly, write the correct spelling of the word on the line.

6. monkies   _____

7. trolleys   _____

8. poppies   _____

9. spys   _____

10. bays   _____

Spelling Patterns and Exceptions Review

Minute 91

Name _____

Draw a line through unnecessary negative words. Write another word on the line to replace it if needed.

1. That new restaurant on Highway 90 will not get no business. _____

2. Nobody travels on that road barely at all. _____

3. It won't get hardly no business because it's too secluded. _____

4. They didn't even put no signs out to let people know they are there! _____

5. My family and I ate there once, and there weren't no other customers there but us. _____

6. Nobody thought the food was not delicious. _____

7. Mr. Anderson said he thought the restaurant wouldn't stay in business neither. _____

8. The owner said she didn't need no help advertising. _____

9. She wasn't putting up no billboards because they're expensive. _____

10. She hardly had no money for the advertising budget. _____

Grammar Minutes · Grade 6 © 2009 Creative Teaching Press

Minute 92

Name _____

For Numbers 1–8, draw a line from each part of speech to its definition.

1. verb   **a.** modifies a verb, adjective, or other adverb

2. noun   **b.** takes the place of a noun

3. adjective   **c.** modifies a noun

4. adverb   **d.** expresses strong feeling

5. conjunction   **e.** joins words or groups of words

6. interjection   **f.** names a person, place, or thing

7. preposition   **g.** shows how two things are related

8. pronoun   **h.** tells the action in a sentence

For Number 9, circle the examples of adverbs.

9. always   unappetizing   frustrate   really   startle

For Number 10, circle the examples of prepositions.

10. under   tomorrow   too   to   west

Grammar Minutes · Grade 6 © 2009 Creative Teaching Press

Minute 93

Name _____

Insert punctuation marks (commas, apostrophes, quotation marks, and end punctuation) for each sentence.

1. Would you like to dance

2. Look out for that fly ball

3. I did my homework already

4. Jason please don't interrupt

5. Martie said You are a good actor

6. Please get eggs milk and cereal from the store

7. Mr Wall cant make his appointment with Dr Smith

8. Oops I dropped my ice-cream cone

9. Clean your room Mom commanded

10. Do you always watch that show

Grammar Minutes · Grade 6 © 2009 Creative Teaching Press

Minute 94

Name _____

For Numbers 1–5, circle the misused word and write it correctly on the line.

1. Did you're sister make the volleyball team?   _____

2. There going to Smithville for a tournament on Saturday.   _____

3. You look ill. Would you like to lay down?   _____

4. Your going to do well on that test!   _____

5. Please sit the mail on that desk.   _____

For Numbers 6–10, insert the correct punctuation at the end of each sentence. Then write the type of sentence it is on the line. Write *D* for declarative, *I* for interrogative, *IMP* for imperative, or *E* for exclamatory.

6. Where should we go for dinner____   _____

7. We should go to Market City Restaurant for dinner____   _____

8. Bring cash, because the restaurant doesn't accept credit cards____   _____

9. I wish I could order two pieces of the cheesecake for dessert____   _____

10. I can't believe how much I just ate____   _____

Apply Your Grammar Knowledge

Minute 95

Name _____

Circle *singular, plural, singular possessive,* or *plural possessive* to describe the boldfaced noun in each sentence.

1. Renee loves to watch the **horses** run and play.

    singular   plural   singular possessive   plural possessive

2. The young **foal** follows its mother everywhere.

    singular   plural   singular possessive   plural possessive

3. Two playful **ponies** whinny and snicker.

    singular   plural   singular possessive   plural possessive

4. The **ponies'** movements are swift and graceful.

    singular   plural   singular possessive   plural possessive

5. That **horse's** mane is braided.

    singular   plural   singular possessive   plural possessive

6. **Snowflake's** stall has been cleaned out.

    singular   plural   singular possessive   plural possessive

7. Snowflake will have a new **colt** soon.

    singular   plural   singular possessive   plural possessive

8. Renee used to exercise Snowflake on the **trails** behind the house.

    singular   plural   singular possessive   plural possessive

9. She also keeps the barn stocked full of carrots, the **animals'** favorite treat.

    singular   plural   singular possessive   plural possessive

10. The magnificent **stallion's** coat is shiny and black.

    singular   plural   singular possessive   plural possessive

Grammar Minutes · Grade 6 © 2009 Creative Teaching Press

Minute 96

Name _____

For Numbers 1–5, circle *adjective* **or** *adverb* **to describe the boldfaced words in each sentence.**

1. Jana **sharply** scolded the child for running into the street.

     adjective   adverb

2. "The cars come **fast,** and they can't see you!" she admonished.

     adjective   adverb

3. The **sheepish** child hung his head.

     adjective   adverb

4. Then he looked at Jana with **teary** eyes.

     adjective   adverb

5. Jana could see that he felt **embarrassed**.

     adjective   adverb

For Numbers 6–10, underline the verb and write *past, present,* **or** *future* **on the line to describe when the action takes place.**

6. Trina helps her sister get dressed. _____

7. Dad had called to see if Aunt Sue was okay. _____

8. Marie has packed for her camping trip. _____

9. Matthew will get a puppy by the end of the week. _____

10. Kelly went to the store for groceries. _____

Apply Your Grammar Knowledge

Minute 97

Name _____

Circle *simple, compound, complex,* or *compound-complex* to describe the structure of each sentence.

1. Thomas Edison was a famous inventor.

      simple   compound   complex   compound-complex

2. Benjamin Franklin was an inventor, but he was also a statesman.

      simple   compound   complex   compound-complex

3. He invented things that improved people's lives.

      simple   compound   complex   compound-complex

4. Some inventors are not even trying to invent anything, but they stumble onto a brilliant idea out of necessity or by accident.

      simple   compound   complex   compound-complex

5. When an ice-cream vendor ran out of dishes at the World's Fair, he used rolled-up wafers from a neighboring stall to make ice-cream cones.

      simple   compound   complex   compound-complex

6. People loved the idea, and they probably always will!

      simple   compound   complex   compound-complex

7. Some inventions make life much easier.

      simple   compound   complex   compound-complex

8. The Internet has made research and access to information very simple.

      simple   compound   complex   compound-complex

9. George Washington Carver was an agricultural chemist who discovered three hundred uses for peanuts.

      simple   compound   complex   compound-complex

10. Alexander Graham Bell invented the telephone.

      simple   compound   complex   compound-complex

Grammar Minutes · Grade 6 © 2009 Creative Teaching Press

Minute 98

Name _____

Circle the dependent clause in each sentence. Then write *complex* or *compound-complex* after each sentence.

1. Mr. Bert loves to work in the flower garden, but he doesn't get to enjoy it very often because he spends so much time at work.

_____

2. If he neglects the shrubs, they become bushy and look messy.

_____

3. Though Mr. Bert usually prefers colorful roses, he planted some fragrant gardenias, and he enjoyed them very much.

_____

4. Sometimes Mr. Bert puts off weeding the garden, so he has lots of work to do when he finally gets around to it.

_____

5. Mr. Bert sits in the garden that is located in his yard.

_____

6. All kinds of creatures visit Mr. Bert's yard because he places birdbaths and feeders in strategic locations.

_____

7. Hummingbirds often feed on the honeysuckle, and Mr. Bert's children love to watch them as the tiny birds zip from flower to flower.

_____

8. Mr. Bert also grows herbs in his garden, and Mrs. Bert uses them when she is cooking special meals.

_____

9. Mr. Bert wants his children to garden, though they don't seem interested.

_____

10. Mr. Bert thought his yard looked nice, but his neighbors, who were impressed with his gardening talents, thought it was spectacular.

_____

Grammar Minutes · Grade 6 © 2009 Creative Teaching Press

Apply Your Grammar Knowledge

Minute 99

Name _____

Circle the verb that agrees with the subject to complete each sentence.

1. Jack and Donna (was, were) surprised they won the three-legged race.

2. Tigers (is, are) beautiful animals.

3. July (is, are) our hottest month in this city.

4. Destiny (love, loves) to sew.

5. Rafts and inner tubes (is, are) available to rent if you want to take a trip down the river.

6. Neither of the two ovens (is, are) working.

7. There (is, are) no good reason to sit back and do nothing.

8. One-third of the students (was, were) present at the play.

9. One of the students (was, were) ill.

10. The principal (decide, decides) what will happen next.

Grammar Minutes · Grade 6 © 2009 Creative Teaching Press

Minute 100

Name _____

Write new words that contain the Greek or Latin root words.

1. aqua _____

2. dia _____

3. herb _____

4. derm _____

5. ped _____

6. fix _____

7. struct _____

8. scrib _____

9. bio _____

10. hydro _____

Grammar Minutes • Grade 6 © 2009 Creative Teaching Press

Apply Your Grammar Knowledge

Minute Answer Key

Minute 1
1. C
2. I
3. I
4. C
5. C
6. I
7. C
8. C
9. I
10. C

Minute 2
1. ., declarative
2. ?, interrogative
3. !, exclamatory
4. ., declarative
5. ?, interrogative
6. ., declarative
7. ., declarative
8. ., imperative
9. ! or ., exclamatory
10. ., imperative

Minute 3
1. circle: teacher
   underline: Our eager classroom teacher
2. circle: marker
   underline: The yellow marker
3. circle: problem
   underline: The algebra problem
4. circle: students
   underline: The students, including my best friend,
5. circle: you
   underline: you
6. circle: asked
   underline: asked Tyson to demonstrate how to solve the problem
7. circle: solved
   underline: solved the problem by working backwards
8. circle: were
   underline: were the only ones to correctly answer the problem
9. circle: tried
   underline: tried to work through the problem again
10. circle: use
    underline: use a different method

Minute 4
1. puppy, pound
2. name, pet
3. dog, collar
4. argument, choices
5. puppy, bear
6. fight, suggestion
7. mother, alternative
8. problem, creature
9. chase, kids
10. friend, tail

Minute 5
1. circle: dog, coat
   underline: Remy
2. circle: groomer
   underline: Furry Friends Grooming Shop
3. circle: fur
   underline: None
4. circle: worker, claws, ears
   underline: Henry
5. circle: friend
   underline: Trixie
6. circle: collar, neck
   underline: None
7. circle: dogs, treats, behavior
   underline: None
8. circle: dogs, hands, face
   underline: None
9. circle: canines, home
   underline: None
10. circle: pet, shop
    underline: Highland Boulevard

Minute 6
1. babies, blankets
2. pets, people
3. coworkers, friends
4. twins, cats
5. families, felines
6. patches, homes
7. haunches, toes
8. games, leaves
9. neighbors, women
10. wishes, dogs

Minute 7
1. churches
2. trees
3. countries
4. buses
5. babies
6. deer
7. shelves
8. geese
9. beliefs
10. children

Minute 8
1. dog's toy
2. baby's bottle
3. Trevor's baseball
4. bee's stinger
5. puppy's tail
6. bird's wing
7. your mother's car
8. bus's back tire
9. deer's tracks
10. Mom's new haircut

Minute 9
1. cheerleaders' uniforms
2. football players' helmets
3. trumpeters' horns
4. marching bands' performances
5. people's cheers
6. teams' coaches
7. mascots' uniforms
8. football parents' cakes and pies
9. fans' umbrellas
10. rivals' taunts

Minute 10
1. You
2. They
3. He
4. She
5. We
6. them
7. us
8. her
9. me
10. him

Minute 11
1. ?
2. I
3. .
4. !
5. I
6. .
7. ?
8. .
9. I
10. ?

Minute 12
1. underline: winter
   circle: Stephen, Washington, D.C.
2. underline: grandfather, cousin
   circle: Joseph
3. underline: None
   circle: Washington Monument, Lincoln Memorial
4. underline: None
   circle: Papa Joe, Vietnam Veterans Memorial
5. underline: dome
   circle: United States Capitol, National Mall
6. underline: city
   circle: Stephen, Gallaudet University
7. underline: None
   circle: Stephen, Joseph, Pennsylvania Avenue
8. underline: photos, president
   circle: White House
9. underline: flag
   circle: Stephen, United States
10. underline: postcards
    circle: Joseph, Oval Office, *USS Philadelphia*

Minute 13
1. people
2. cherries
3. cactus
4. industries
5. sheep
6. scarf
7. women
8. vertebrae
9. parenthesis
10. calves

Minute 14
1. plural possessive
2. singular possessive
3. plural possessive
4. singular possessive
5. plural possessive
6. men's oars
7. islands' shores
8. people's nets
9. tribes' customs
10. waves' crests

Minute 15
1. him
2. us
3. She
4. they
5. We
6. them
7. You
8. it
9. I
10. He

Minute 16
Answers will vary. Sample answers include:
1. bake
2. writes
3. drives
4. chooses
5. finds
6. takes
7. heads
8. cleans
9. follows
10. tops

Minute 17
1. was
2. became
3. seem
4. feel
5. am
6. be
7. were
8. is
9. are
10. feel

Minute 18
1. am
2. are
3. have
4. is
5. might
6. was
7. will
8. would
9. does
10. has

Minute 19
1. do—present tense
2. cleaned—past tense
3. helped—past tense
4. will help—future tense
5. plan—present tense
6. will water—future tense
7. forgot—past tense
8. try—present tense
9. will get—future tense
10. save—present tense

Minute 20
1. had packed—past perfect
2. had planned—past perfect
3. will have canceled—future perfect

Minute Answer Key

4. has called—present perfect
5. has broken—present perfect
6. has said; will have said
7. had regretted; has regretted
8. had lounged; will have lounged
9. had assured; will have assured
10. has expressed; will have expressed

Minute 21
1. ate
2. bite
3. forgotten
4. broke
5. written
6. bleed
7. undid
8. spread
9. feel
10. given

Minute 22
1. are expecting—present progressive
2. are staying—present progressive
3. were planning—past progressive
4. will be entertaining—future progressive
5. was encouraging—past progressive
6. am thinking
7. is helping
8. are creating
9. is saying
10. am looking

Minute 23
1. loves→grandparents
2. know→things
3. collects→coins
4. tells→history
5. builds→sailboats
6. showed→masterpiece
7. writes→poetry
8. sends→verses
9. enjoy→reading
10. memorizes→rhymes

Minute 24
1. blew—how
2. hid—where
3. creaked and moaned
4. rattled
5. fell—how
6. died—when
7. ended—when
8. went—where
9. stepped—how
10. gathered—where

Minute 25
1. doesn't
2. love
3. order
4. asks

5. does
6. eats
7. prefer
8. are
9. does
10. shakes

Minute 26
Order of answers may vary.
1. read
2. travel
3. listen
4. save
5. gather
6. eat
7. breathe
8. think
9. recognize
10. dance

Minute 27
1. became—linking
2. was trying—helping
3. was watching—helping
4. was—linking
5. was running—helping
6. felt—linking
7. was—linking
8. were hoping—helping
9. were relaxing—helping
10. was—linking

Minute 28
1. swim
2. had crawled
3. drink
4. had broken
5. have grown
6. will have walked
7. had fallen
8. have hit
9. will have grabbed
10. had crushed

Minute 29
1. transitive
2. intransitive
3. intransitive
4. transitive
5. transitive
6. transitive
7. intransitive
8. transitive
9. intransitive
10. intransitive

Minute 30
1. sleep
2. try
3. gets
4. is
5. eat
6. feels
7. plan
8. has
9. want
10. are

Minute 31
1. spectacular→zoo
2. sunny→weather beautiful→day

3. first→animals scaly→reptiles
4. giant→elephants
5. hairy→elephants
6. warm→hut tropical→plants
7. loose→hummingbirds
8. busy→birds sugary→nectar
9. large→cats favorite→sight
10. playful→cubs

Minute 32
1. funnier, funniest
2. more expensive, most expensive
3. longer, longest
4. sicker, sickest
5. smaller, smallest
6. quicker, quickest
7. more exciting, most exciting
8. hotter, hottest
9. more colorful, most colorful
10. prettier, prettiest

Minute 33
Comparative	Superlative
1. better	2. best
3. worse	4. worst
5. farther or further	6. farthest or furthest
7. more	8. most
9. less	10. least

Minute 34
1. boldly—boldly walked
2. calmly—calmly spoke
3. excitedly—excitedly shout
4. nervously—nervously wait
5. loudly—loudly bark
6. easily—easily pass
7. quickly—quickly heals
8. completely—completely finishes
9. busily—busily prepares
10. bravely—bravely jumps

Minute 35
1. happily→agreed
2. fiercely→serves
3. swiftly→flies
4. speedily→reacts
5. soundly→hits
6. barely→misses
7. wildly→swings
8. expertly→returns
9. closely→are matched
10. gladly→will return

Minute 36
1. always→coaches
2. hard→work
3. near→comes

4. fastest→runs
5. farthest→hits
6. often→shouted
7. there→throw
8. close→buzzed
9. again→won
10. well→have done

Minute 37
1. moist
2. ignore
3. discontinue
4. certain
5. grasp
6. imitate
7. faithful
8. angry
9. challenge
10. perplex

Minute 38
1. dry
2. dull
3. give
4. dead
5. simple
6. light
7. often
8. awake
9. smooth
10. busy

Minute 39
1. write (or rite)
2. threw
3. hear
4. meat
5. seem
6. hare
7. bare
8. deer
9. steal
10. role

Minute 40
1. noun
2. comparative
3. superlative
4. better
5. quick
6. shaky
7. helpful
8. advanced
9. winning
10. undefeated

Minute 41
1. shorter
2. worse
3. curliest
4. lonelier
5. cuter
6. bigger, biggest
7. littler/less, littlest/least
8. more, most
9. sleepier, sleepiest
10. better, best

Minute Answer Key

Minute 42
1. always→go camping
2. usually→rains
3. here→pitch
4. closer→camp
5. patiently→waited
6. deftly→cleaned
7. carefully→lit
8. happily→ate
9. cautiously→hiked
10. leisurely→admired

Minute 43
1. S	6. A
2. A	7. S
3. S	8. S
4. A	9. S
5. A	10. A

Minute 44
1. pail	6. kneaded
2. weather	7. piece
3. there	8. would
4. too	9. you're
5. flour	10. sea

Minute 45
1. however	6. except
2. so	7. or
3. and	8. yet
4. or	9. so
5. but	10. and

Minute 46
1. None
2. She and her friends
3. Lemon custard and butter pecan
4. Chocolate sprinkles, walnuts, or chocolate chips
5. None
6. None
7. None
8. Sundaes and milkshakes
9. Annie and Sandy
10. None

Minute 47
1. tumbles and dives
2. dreams and believes
3. None
4. thinks and ponders
5. None
6. None
7. None
8. have been and have worked
9. None
10. encourage and tell

Minute 48
1. before
2. after
3. during

4. near
5. to
6. in the yard
7. across the grass
8. between the houses
9. into the alley
10. up a telephone pole

Minute 49
For Numbers 1–5, order of answers may vary.
1. when the cake was served
2. if you need my opinion
3. because I was tired
4. and if I remember correctly
5. until the police arrived
6. who does not have a dog
7. what happened yesterday
8. Wherever Mason goes
9. If you agree to help
10. that has the white patches

Minute 50
For Numbers 1–5, order of answers may vary.
1. I know Mr. Fletcher
2. Maria is a letter carrier
3. please pass the potatoes
4. the sun came up
5. carry the boxes
6. Thomas is a veterinarian
7. They care for animals
8. they help sick pets
9. People count on them
10. I want to be like them

Minute 51
1. siblings, they
2. differ, so
3. comedies, talk shows, and action shows, but Linda likes dramas, detective shows, and
4. argue, but
5. involved, although
6. other, and
7. parents, so
8. watch, and
9. shows, but
10. happy, and

Minute 52
1. No	6. Yes
2. No	7. No
3. Yes	8. Yes
4. No	9. Yes
5. Yes	10. No

Minute 53
1. No	6. Yes
2. Yes	7. Yes
3. Yes	8. Yes

4. Yes	9. No
5. No	10. No

Minute 54
1. Giovanna joined the marching band, but Selma, who was more athletic, joined the basketball team.
2. Giovanna thought that Selma was making a mistake, but Selma, who is usually indecisive, was sure of her decision.
3. The girls were sad not to be in the same classes, but they both looked forward to new experiences because they spent all their time together.
4. Since the school year started, the girls barely saw each other, and they missed their close friendship.
5. They got together on weekends, and they talked about everything that came to mind.
6. Giovanna and Selma supported each other, but they didn't agree about all things like which extra-curricular activity to join.
7. Even though the girls didn't see each other often, they remained friends and they introduced one another to new people.
8. Giovanna and Selma were both hard workers, and they excelled at their talents, which made their parents proud.
9. Giovanna, who had joined the drum section, played the cadence at Selma's basketball games, and the crowd loved it.
10. The cadence sparked energy in the team, so they played better when the drum section was there.

Minute 55
For Numbers 1–5, order of answers may vary.
1. but
2. because
3. so

4. however
5. and
6. but
7. or
8. so
9. yet
10. and

Minute 56
1. compound predicate
2. compound predicate
3. compound subject
4. compound predicate
5. compound subject
6. compound predicate
7. compound subject
8. compound subject
9. compound predicate
10. compound subject

Minute 57
1. behind
2. after
3. near
4. inside
5. before
For numbers 6–10 answers will vary. Sample answers include:
6. to the playhouse
7. by the creek
8. against the wall
9. about school
10. in the yard

Minute 58
1. dependent clause
2. independent clause
3. independent clause
4. dependent clause
5. independent clause
6. independent clause
7. dependent clause
8. independent clause
9. independent clause
10. dependent clause

Minute 59
1. independent clauses
2. independent clause
3. dependent clauses
4. independent clauses
5. dependent clauses
6. a
7. b
8. a
9. c
10. a

Minute 60
1. the mountain with the highest altitude in the world
2. or 8,848 meters
3. one of the first men to climb Mount Everest

Minute Answer Key

4. a Japanese mountain climber
5. or reaching the top of a mountain
6. or deaths
7. an inactive volcano in Hawaii
8. the second highest mountain on earth
9. Mount McKinley
10. or 6,193.6 meters

Minute 61
1. June 15, 1996.
2. eat pizza, go bowling, and
3. birthday, he
4. hot, humid
5. party, weren't
6. said, "Ren, you
7. answered, "Don't worry, Dad!"
8. Anaheim, California, on
9. says, "Celebrating
10. now, he

Minute 62
1. "Have you ever seen a manatee?" I asked Don.
2. None
3. None
4. "Oh!" he exclaimed. "I have read about them."
5. "Don't they live in waters off the coast of Texas and Florida?" he asked.
6. "Yes, but manatees are endangered," I answered.
7. None
8. "I read that they are sometimes called sea cows," Don added.
9. "Ben lives in Florida, and he sees them sometimes," I said.
10. "What other marine life is endangered?" Don asked.

Minute 63
1. they are—they're
2. should have—should've
3. You will—You'll
4. It is—It's
5. we will—we'll
6. they would—they'd
7. Does not—Doesn't
8. Do not—Don't
9. are not—aren't
10. You have—You've

Minute 64
1. Mr.   6. Capt.
2. Mrs.   7. Ave.
3. Jr.   8. St.
4. Sen.   9. Blvd.
5. Dr.   10. Hwy.

Minute 65
1. accident; however
2. lines; therefore
3. slipped; then
4. horse; however
5. car; therefore
6. play; indeed
7. mistake; besides
8. teacher; however
9. road; indeed
10. States; however

Minute 66
1. greeting
2. list
3. dialogue
4. ingredients: yeast
5. Jason: Hi Kathleen!
6. suggestions: First
7. Sir: We
8. supplies: scissors
9. Concern: I
10. address: 227

Minute 67
1. set   6. sit
2. sit   7. set
3. set   8. sit
4. set   9. Set
5. sit   10. set

Minute 68
1. lay   6. lie
2. lie   7. lie
3. lay   8. lay
4. lay   9. lie
5. lie   10. lay

Minute 69
1. you're   6. Your
2. Your   7. your
3. your   8. you're
4. your   9. your
5. You're   10. you're

Minute 70
1. the capital of Texas
2. the capital of the United States
3. the first state to ratify the U.S. Constitution
4. the Peach State
5. Alaska's capital city
6. the Sunshine State
7. the Great Lakes State
8. the Constitution State
9. the Empire State
10. now called the Golden State

Minute 71
1. "What type of books do you like to read?" Mrs. Turner asked me.
2. "I like to read mysteries, historical fiction, and poetry," I replied.

3. She said that I could borrow her books, and she helped me choose the first one.
4. It was a fictional story about a girl who lived in Atlanta, Georgia, during the Civil War.
5. When I was finished with it, I asked Mrs. Turner, "May I borrow another?"
6. She replied, "Of course you may."
7. "Carlie, you should keep a journal and write notes about all the books you read," Mrs. Turner suggested.
8. I wrote in a journal every night, and soon I began to have ideas about stories I could write.
9. The more I wrote, the stronger my writing became.
10. I enjoy reading and writing more than ever now, thanks to Mrs. Turner.

Minute 72
1. We are—We're
2. you are—you're
3. it is—it's
4. could have—could've
5. we would—we'd
6. Captain
7. Senator
8. Boulevard
9. Mister
10. Highway

Minute 73
1. C
2. C
3. S
4. S
5. C
6. late; then
7. store: eggs
8. address: 1999
9. one; therefore
10. steps: first

Minute 74
1. Your   6. set
2. lie   7. your
3. set   8. lie
4. You're   9. You're
5. sit   10. lie

Minute 75
1. Hey!   6. Ouch!
2. Oops!   7. Well
3. Oh   8. Oh, no!
4. Help!   9. Whoa!
5. Hooray!   10. Rats!

Minute 76
1. the   6. an
2. a   7. an
3. the   8. the
4. the   9. a
5. a   10. an

Minute 77
Answers may vary. Sample answers include:
1. disassemble
2. nonsense
3. retroactive
4. unattractive
5. multicultural
6. microwave
7. irreversible
8. nondairy
9. antibacterial
10. uncertain

Minute 78
1. kindness
2. happiness
3. weariness
4. softness
5. emptiness
6. intention
7. attention
8. subtraction
9. election
10. creation

Minute 79
Answers may vary. Sample answers include:
1. indirect
2. pretest
3. reappear
4. semicircle
5. autograph
6. deform
7. immobile
8. precaution
9. impossible
10. indecisive

Minute 80
1. foldable
2. washable
3. erasable
4. movable or moveable
5. likable or likeable
6. hopeless
7. fearless
8. senseless
9. friendless
10. careless

Minute 81
1. through or across—diagonal
2. foot—podiatrist
3. time—chronology
4. birth—generation
5. water—hydrate
6. distance—telescope

Minute Answer Key

7. measure—metric
8. book—bibliography
9. life—biology
10. skin—epidermis

Minute 82
1. sun—solar
2. water—aquarium
3. belief—incredible
4. plant—herbivore
5. feet—pedicure
6. earth—territory
7. fasten—affix
8. write—inscribe
9. right—justice
10. build—construct

Minute 83
1. C
2. receive
3. seize
4. believe
5. C
6. retrieve
7. C
8. weird
9. C
10. C

Minute 84
1. monkeys
2. C
3. C
4. C
5. C
6. turkeys
7. C
8. C
9. chimneys
10. journeys

Minute 85
For Numbers 1–5, order of answers may vary.
1. no
2. barely
3. nowhere
4. nobody
5. neither
6. I
7. C
8. I
9. I
10. C

Minute 86
For Numbers 1–5, answers may vary. Sample answers include:
1. Hey
2. Ouch
3. Well
4. Rats
5. Oh
6. the
7. a
8. an
9. the
10. an

Minute 87
Answers may vary. Sample answers include:
1. not poisonous
2. not flexible
3. self-written life story
4. a tiny chip or device

5. to take something apart so it's not connected
6. to see beforehand
7. not truthful
8. many uses
9. every half year
10. not able to be done

Minute 88
Answers may vary. Sample answers include:
1. darkness
2. fascination
3. narration
4. thoughtless
5. worthiness
6. restlessness
7. comfortable
8. senseless
9. weariness
10. agreeable

Minute 89
1. foot
2. time
3. far away
4. life
5. skin
6. build
7. write
8. sun
9. earth
10. right

Minute 90
1. cieling
2. frieght
3. peirce
4. sieze
5. nieghbor
6. monkeys
7. C
8. C
9. spies
10. C

Minute 91
Answers may vary. Sample answers include:
1. will ~~not~~ get (hardly) ~~no~~ (any) business
2. that road ~~barely~~ at all.
3. get hardly ~~no~~ (any) business
4. put ~~no~~ signs
5. there weren't ~~no~~ (any)
6. ~~Nobody~~ (Everybody) thought the food was ~~not~~ delicious.
7. business ~~neither~~.
8. need ~~no~~ help
9. up ~~no~~ billboards
10. She ~~hardly~~ had no money

Minute 92
1. h
2. f
3. c
4. a
5. e
6. d

7. g
8. b
9. always, really
10. under, to

Minute 93
1. dance?
2. ball!
3. already.
4. Jason, please don't interrupt!
5. Martie said, "You are a good actor."
6. eggs, milk, and cereal from the store.
7. Mr. Wall can't make his appointment with Dr. Smith.
8. Oops! I dropped my ice-cream cone!
9. "Clean your room!" Mom commanded.
10. Do you always watch that show?

Minute 94
1. your
2. They're
3. lie
4. You're
5. set
6. ?, I
7. ., D
8. ., IMP
9. ., D
10. !, E

Minute 95
1. plural
2. singular
3. plural
4. plural possessive
5. singular possessive
6. singular possessive
7. singular
8. plural
9. plural possessive
10. singular possessive

Minute 96
1. adverb
2. adverb
3. adjective
4. adjective
5. adjective
6. helps—present
7. had called, was—past
8. has packed—past
9. will get—future
10. went—past

Minute 97
1. simple
2. compound
3. complex
4. compound-complex
5. complex
6. compound
7. simple
8. simple
9. complex
10. simple

Minute 98
1. circle: because he spends so much time at work—compound-complex
2. circle: If he neglects the shrubs—complex
3. circle: Though Mr. Bert usually prefers color-ful roses—compound-complex
4. circle: when he finally gets around to it—com-pound-complex
5. circle: that is located in his yard—complex
6. circle: because he places birdbaths and feeders in strategic locations—complex
7. circle: as the tiny birds zip from flower to flow-er—compound-complex
8. circle: when she is cook-ing special meals—com-pound-complex
9. circle: though they don't seem interested—com-plex
10. circle: who were impressed with his gardening talents—com-pound-complex

Minute 99
1. were
2. are
3. is
4. loves
5. are
6. is
7. is
8. were
9. was
10. decides

Minute 100
Answers may vary. Sample answers include:
1. aquatic
2. diameter
3. herbivore
4. epidermis
5. centipede
6. fixture
7. construction
8. scribble
9. biome
10. hydrate